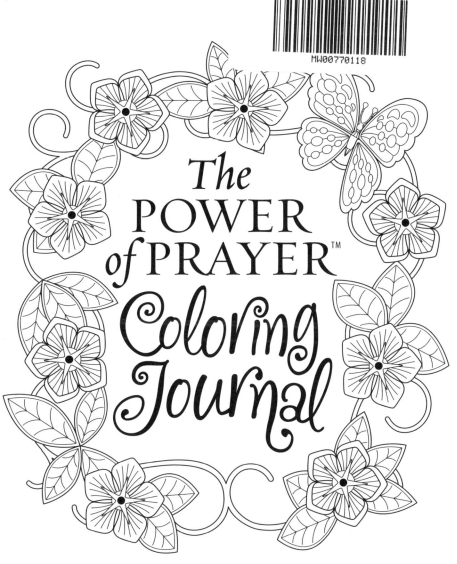

The POWER of PRAYER™
Coloring Journal

STORMIE OMARTIAN

Artwork by Marie Michaels

HARVEST HOUSE PUBLISHERS
EUGENE, OREGON

Cover by Dugan Design Group

THE POWER OF PRAYER™ COLORING JOURNAL
copyright ©2017 by Stormie Omartian, Artwork ©2017 by Dugan Design Group
Published by Harvest House Publishers
Eugene, Oregon 97402

www.harvesthousepublishers.com

ISBN 978-0-7369-7014-3

Printed in the United States of America

20 21 22 23 24 25 /VP/ 6 5 4 3 2

Introduction

There is something memorable about filling in an art design with color. It becomes imprinted on your mind in a peaceful and impactful way. Thirty-five prayers are included in this special coloring book for adults, and each one is captured on four pages. The first page on the left is the prayer. The second page on the right is simply the title of the prayer, which is itself a shortened prayer. The third page is there for you to journal your specific prayers, concerns, and insights with regard to that prayer. As you share your personal thoughts and feelings with God, you can also write down anything He impresses upon your heart. The fourth page is the verse that supports or inspires the prayer.

You can use colored pencils or crayons or whatever you like. There is no right or wrong way to do this. Just find time for peace and calm in the midst of your busy day, a place for intimate communication between you and God. Let Him inspire you with the gifts He has put in you. This is your own creative expression to Him. I pray you will sense the beautiful and rejuvenating peace of God every time you open this book.

Stormie Omartian

Lord, may Your Word remind me of who You are and how much You love me. May it bring the security of knowing my life is in Your hands and You will supply all my needs. Thank You, Lord, that when I look into Your Word I find You. Give me ears to recognize Your voice speaking to me every time I read it (Mark 4:23). When I hear Your voice and follow You, my life is full. When I get off the path You have for me, my life is empty. Guide, perfect, and fill me with Your Word this day. In Jesus' name I pray.

My Prayer

Lord, take me deeper in Your Word. ....

....

....

....

....

....

....

....

....

....

....

....

....

....

....

....

Blessed are those who keep His testimonies, who seek Him with the whole heart!

PSALM 119:2

Lord, there is no source of greater joy for me than worshiping You. I come into Your presence with thanksgiving and bow before You this day. I exalt Your name, for You are great and worthy to be praised. "You have put gladness in my heart" (Psalm 4:7). All honor and majesty, strength and glory, holiness and righteousness are Yours, O Lord. You are "gracious and full of compassion, slow to anger and great in mercy" (Psalm 145:8). You are "mighty in power" and Your "understanding is infinite" (Psalm 147:5).

You give food to the hungry and freedom to the prisoners. Thank You that You open the eyes of the blind and raise up those who are bowed down (Psalm 146:7-8). In Jesus' name I pray.

My Prayer

Lord, help me to worship You. ....

....

....

....

....

....

....

....

....

....

....

....

....

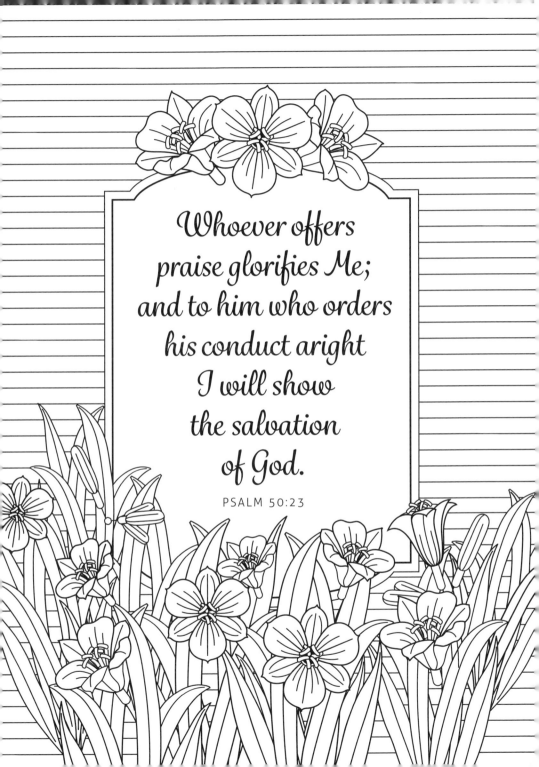

Whoever offers
praise glorifies Me;
and to him who orders
his conduct aright
I will show
the salvation
of God.

PSALM 50:23

LORD, I thank You for the abilities

You have given me. Where I am lacking in skill, help me to grow and improve so that I do my work well. Open doors of opportunity to use my skills, and close doors that I am not to go through. Give me wisdom and direction about that. I commit my work to You, Lord, knowing You will establish it (Proverbs 16:3). May it always be that I love the work I do and am able to do the work I love. Establish the work of my hands so that what I do will find favor with others and be a blessing for many. May it always be glorifying to You. In Jesus' name I pray.

My Prayer

Lord, bless me in the work I do. ....
....
....
....
....
....
....
....
....
....
....
....
....
....
....
....

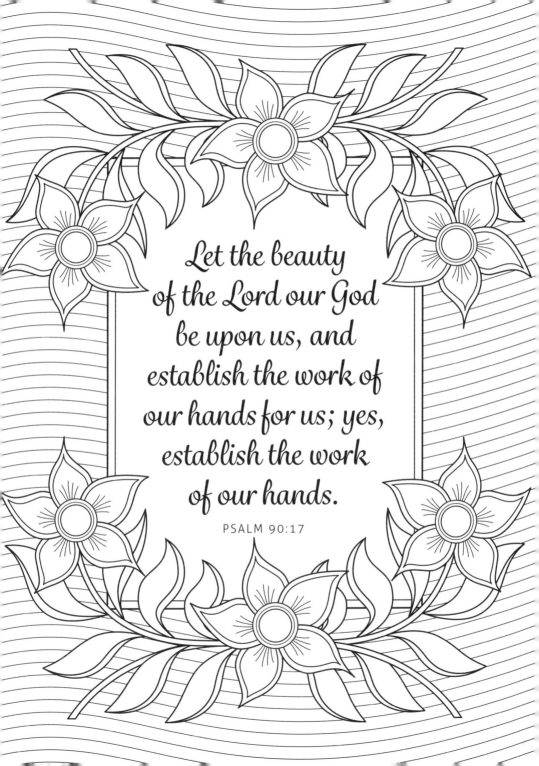

Let the beauty of the Lord our God be upon us, and establish the work of our hands for us; yes, establish the work of our hands.

PSALM 90:17

Lord, I pray You would give me Your wisdom and understanding in all things. I know wisdom is better than gold and understanding is better than silver (Proverbs 16:16), so make me rich in wisdom and wealthy in understanding. Thank You that You give "wisdom to the wise and knowledge to those who have understanding" (Daniel 2:21). Increase my wisdom and knowledge so I can see Your truth in every situation. Give me discernment for each decision I must make. Please help me to always seek godly counsel and not look to the world and ungodly people for answers. Thank You, Lord, that You will give me the counsel and instruction I need, even as I sleep. In Jesus' name I pray.

My Prayer

Lord, give me Your wisdom. ....

....

....

....

....

....

....

....

....

....

....

....

....

....

....

....

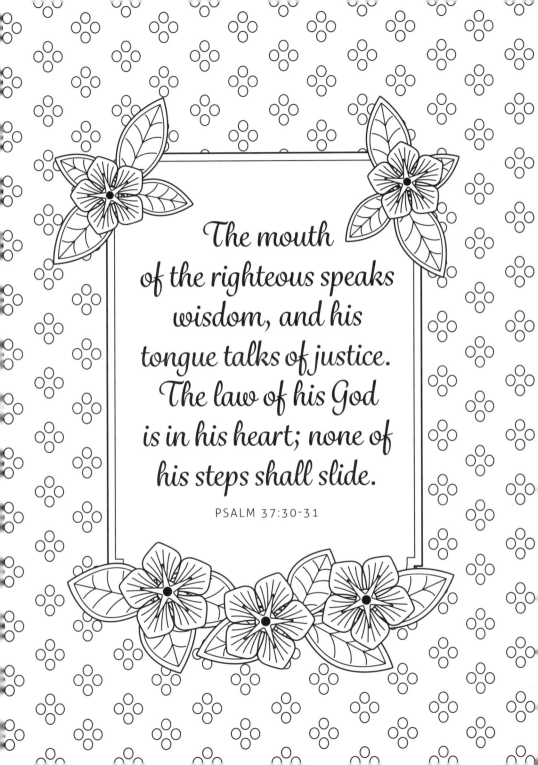

The mouth
of the righteous speaks
wisdom, and his
tongue talks of justice.
The law of his God
is in his heart; none of
his steps shall slide.

PSALM 37:30-31

Lord, Your Word says that those of us who love Your law will have great peace and nothing will cause us to stumble (Psalm 119:165). I love Your law because I know it is good and it is there for my benefit. Enable me to live in obedience to each part of it so that I will not stumble and fall. Help me to obey You so that I can dwell in the confidence and peace of knowing I am living Your way. My heart wants to obey You in all things, Lord. Please show me where I am not doing that. "With my whole heart I have sought You; oh, let me not wander from Your commandments!" (Psalm 119:10). In Jesus' name I pray.

My Prayer

Lord, teach me to walk in obedience. ....

....

....

....

....

....

....

....

....

....

....

....

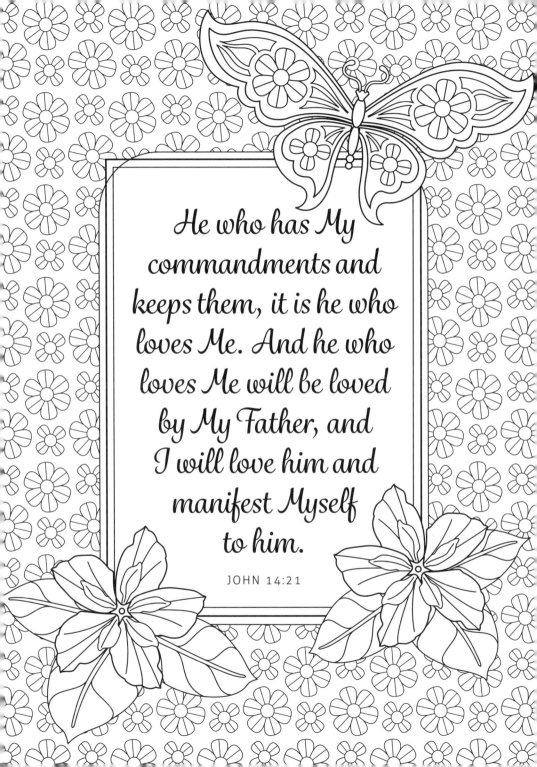

He who has My commandments and keeps them, it is he who loves Me. And he who loves Me will be loved by My Father, and I will love him and manifest Myself to him.

JOHN 14:21

Lord, help me to serve You the way You want me to. Reveal to me any area of my life where I should be giving to someone right now. Open my eyes to see the need. Give me a generous heart to give to the poor. Help me to be a good steward of the blessings You have given me by sharing what I have with others. Show me whom You want me to extend my hand to at this time. Fill me with Your love for all people, and help me to communicate it in a way that can be clearly perceived. Use me to touch the lives of others with the hope that is in me. In Jesus' name I pray.

My Prayer

Lord, use me to reach out to others. ....

....

....

....

....

....

....

....

....

....

....

....

....

....

....

....

....

....

....

....

By this we know
love, because
He laid down His
life for us.
And we also ought
to lay down
our lives for
the brethren.

I JOHN 3:16

LORD, help me be a person who speaks words that build up and not tear down. Help me to speak life into the situations and people around me, and not death. Fill my heart afresh each day with Your Holy Spirit so that Your love and goodness overflow from my heart and my mouth. Help me to speak only about things that are true, noble, just, pure, lovely, of good report, virtuous, and praiseworthy. Holy Spirit of truth, guide me in all truth. "Let the words of my mouth and the meditation of my heart be acceptable in Your sight, O LORD, my strength and my Redeemer" (Psalm 19:14). May every word I speak reflect Your purity and love. In Jesus' name I pray.

My Prayer

Lord, help me speak words of life. ....
....
....
....
....
....
....
....
....
....
....
....
....
....
....

Righteous lips are the delight of kings, and they love him who speaks what is right.

PROVERBS 16:13

Lord, increase my faith. Teach me how to "walk by faith, not by sight" (2 Corinthians 5:7). Give me strength to stand strong on Your promises and believe Your every word. I know that "faith comes by hearing, and hearing by the word of God" (Romans 10:17). Make my faith increase every time I hear or read Your Word. Increase my faith so that I can pray in power. Help me to believe for Your promises to be fulfilled in me. I pray that the genuineness of my faith, which is more precious than gold that perishes even when it is tested by fire, will be glorifying to You, Lord (1 Peter 1:7). In Jesus' name I pray.

My Prayer

Lord, give me mountain-moving faith. ....

....

....

....

....

....

....

....

....

....

....

....

....

....

....

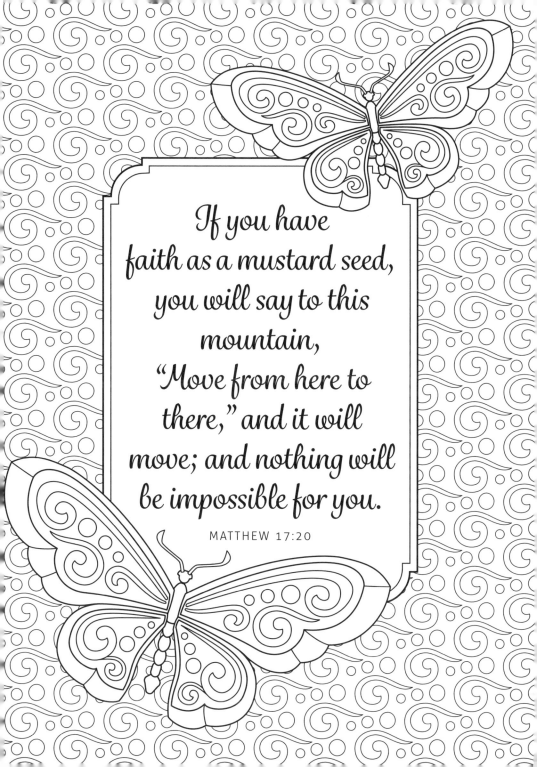

If you have
faith as a mustard seed,
you will say to this
mountain,
"Move from here to
there," and it will
move; and nothing will
be impossible for you.

MATTHEW 17:20

$\mathcal{Lord}$, teach me to love others the way You do. Soften my heart where it has become hard. Make me fresh where I have become stale. Lead me and instruct me where I have become unteachable. Make me to be faithful, giving, and obedient the way Jesus was. Where I am resistant to change, help me to trust Your work in my life. May Your light so shine in me that I become a light to all who know me. May it be not I who lives, but You who lives in me (Galatians 2:20). Make me to be so much like Christ that when people see me they will want to know You better. In Jesus' name I pray.

My Prayer

Lord, change me to be like Christ. ....

....

....

....

....

....

....

....

....

....

....

....

....

....

....

....

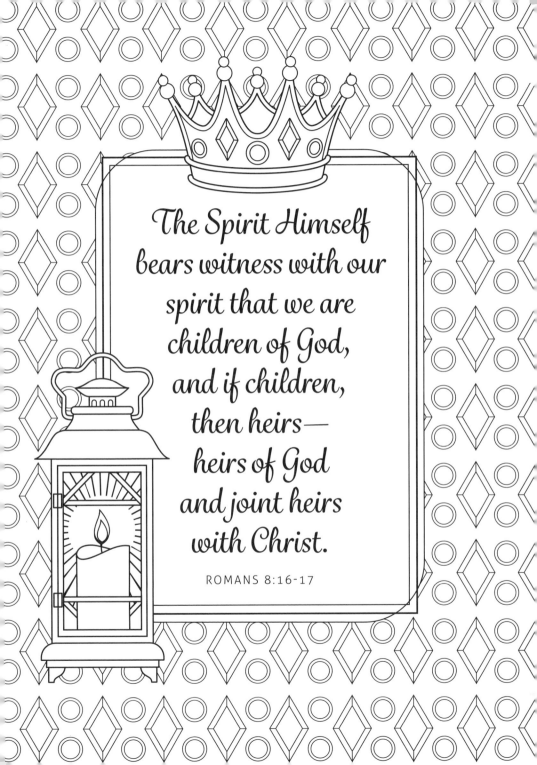

The Spirit Himself bears witness with our spirit that we are children of God, and if children, then heirs— heirs of God and joint heirs with Christ.

ROMANS 8:16-17

Lord, I don't want to take one step without You. I reach up for Your hand and ask that You lead me in Your way. Thank You that no matter where I am right now, even if I have gotten way off course, in this moment as I put my hand in Yours, You will make a path from where I am to where I need to be. And You will lead me on it. I love that Your grace abounds to me in that way. Keep me on the path You have for me and take me where You want me to go. I commit this day to walking with You. In Jesus' name I pray.

My Prayer

Lord, teach me how to walk with You. ....

....

....

....

....

....

....

....

....

....

....

....

....

....

You will show me the path of life; in Your presence is fullness of joy; at Your right hand are pleasures forevermore.

PSALM 16:11

Lord, You are the light of my life. You illuminate my path, and I will follow wherever You lead. Protect me from being blinded by the light that confuses. Help me to always identify the counterfeit. I depend on You to lift up the light of Your countenance upon me (Psalm 4:6). Thank You, Lord, that because You never change, Your light is constant in my life no matter what is going on around me. Shine Your light through me as I walk with my hand in Yours. I give this day to You and trust that the light You give me is just the amount I need for the step I'm on. In Jesus' name I pray.

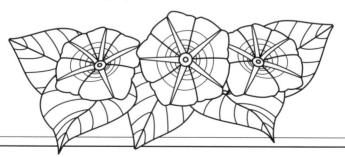

My Prayer

Lord, thank You for Your light.......................................

....

....

....

....

....

....

....

....

....

....

....

....

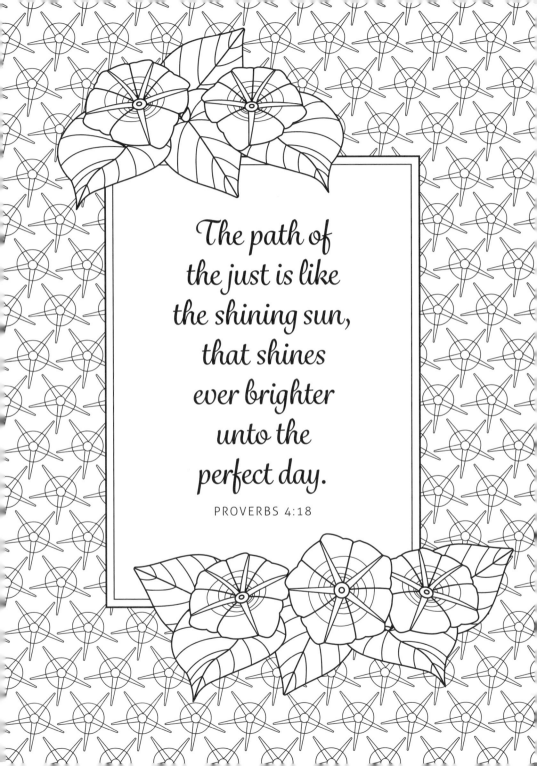

The path of
the just is like
the shining sun,
that shines
ever brighter
unto the
perfect day.

PROVERBS 4:18

LORD,

I regard Your presence and my relationship with You as the most important thing in my life. Help me to never doubt it or take it for granted. In the times when You are testing my faith and my love for You, I pray that I will draw ever closer to You. Even in the most difficult situation of my life right now, I know that You are in control and will turn things around and bring good out of it. I refuse to allow fear or a lack of faith to keep me from walking victoriously in all You have for me. In Jesus' name I pray.

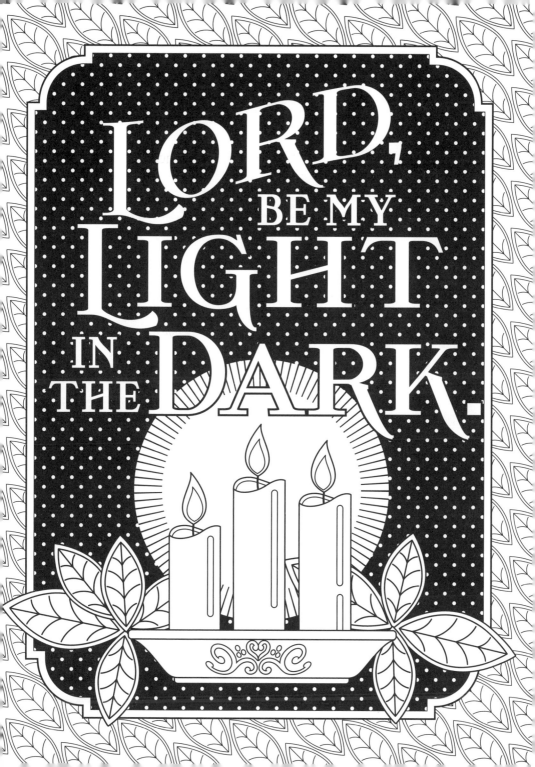

My Prayer

Lord, be my light in the dark. ....

....

....

....

....

....

....

....

....

....

....

....

....

....

....

You will light
my lamp;
the Lord my God
will enlighten
my darkness.

PSALM 18:28

Lord, help me to be content where I am right now on Your path for my life. I know You are always growing me into Your likeness and will not leave me where I am forever. I resolve to see any loneliness or lack of contentment in me as a sign that I need to spend more time with You. Help me to recognize Your blessings and goodness in the midst of every situation I face. Give me strength when I am weary and the fullness of Your joy when I feel sad. Help me to have an ever-increasing faith and a greater sense of Your presence in my life. In Jesus' name I pray.

My Prayer

Lord, help me embrace each moment. ....

....

....

....

....

....

....

....

....

....

....

....

....

....

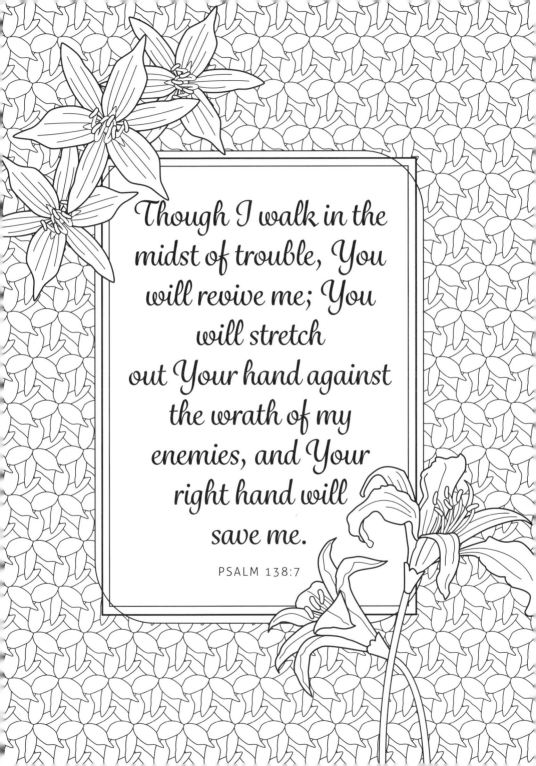

Though I walk in the midst of trouble, You will revive me; You will stretch out Your hand against the wrath of my enemies, and Your right hand will save me.

PSALM 138:7

Lord, shine the light of Your Word on the path of my life today. Make it a lamp for my feet so that I do not stumble. Bring it alive in my spirit so that it illuminates my mind and soul. Let it be a guide for every decision I make, every step I take. Keep me from turning to the right or the left so that I will stay on the narrow path that leads to life. Help me daily to carve out time to be alone with You and to feed on Your truth. In Jesus' name I pray.

My Prayer

Lord, help me to walk safely. ....

....

....

....

....

....

....

....

....

....

....

....

....

....

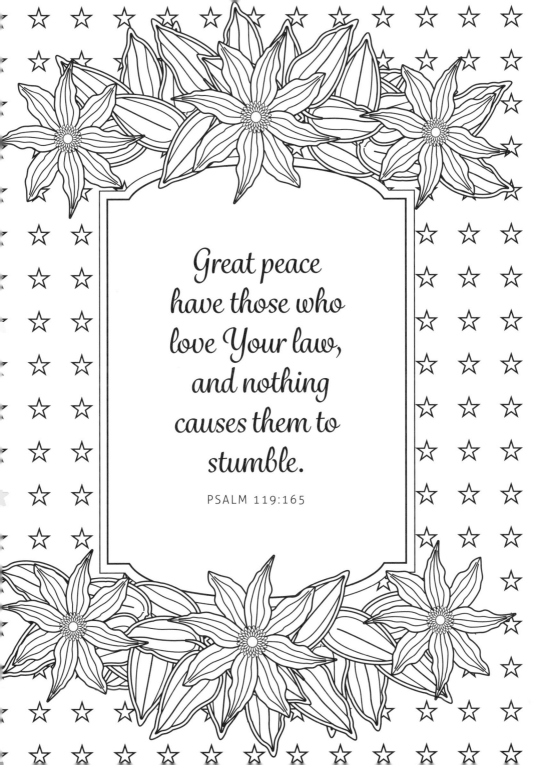

Great peace
have those who
love Your law,
and nothing
causes them to
stumble.

PSALM 119:165

LORD,

grow me up in Your ways and lead me in Your will. Help me to become so strong in You that I will not waver or doubt. Make me to understand Your Word and Your directions to me. "Test me, LORD, and try me, examine my heart and my mind; for I have always been mindful of your unfailing love and have lived in reliance on your faithfulness" (Psalm 26:2-3 NIV). I want to pass successfully through any time of testing You bring me to so that I might be refined.

In Jesus' name I pray.

My Prayer

Lord, test my heart. ....

....

....

....

....

....

....

....

....

....

....

....

....

....

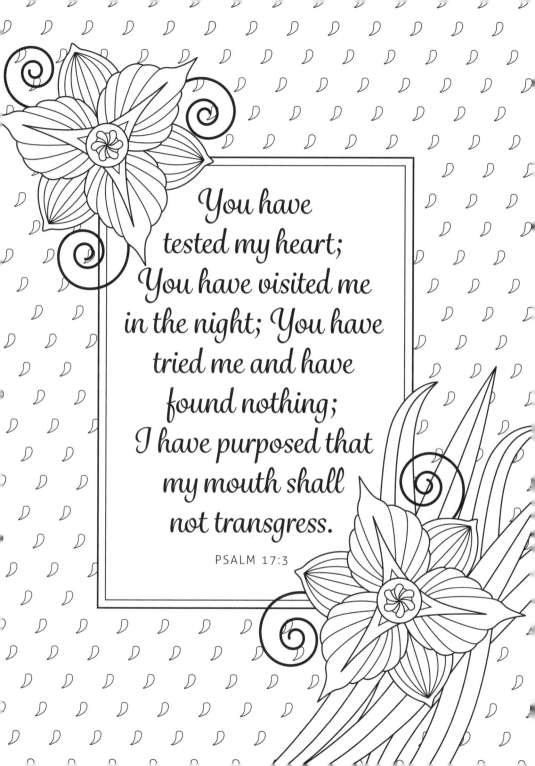

You have
tested my heart;
You have visited me
in the night; You have
tried me and have
found nothing;
I have purposed that
my mouth shall
not transgress.

PSALM 17:3

Lord,

I am at home wherever You are. Shine Your light on the path You have for me to travel, for I know all my days are in Your hands. Forgive me when I grumble or have less than a grateful heart about where I am right now. I realize my attitude will have a direct bearing on whether I wander around in circles or whether I get through to the Promised Land You have for me. Help me to trust You for every step. Enable me to see all the blessings that are right here in this moment. I trust that Your grace is sufficient for this day, and each day that follows. In Jesus' name I pray.

My Prayer

Lord, lead me through the wilderness. ....

....

....

....

....

....

....

....

....

....

....

....

....

....

My sheep
hear My voice,
and
I know them,
and they
follow Me.

JOHN 10:27

Lord, because I want to hear Your voice say, "Well done, My good and faithful servant" when I meet You face-to-face, I will listen to Your voice now. I don't want to be unfruitful and unfulfilled because I never clearly heard Your call. I want You to fill me with Your greatness so that I may do great things for others as You have called me to do. I commit to walking this road step-by-step with You so that I may fully become all that You have made me to be. In Jesus' name I pray.

My Prayer

Lord, help me hear Your voice. ....

....

....

....

....

....

....

....

....

....

....

....

....

....

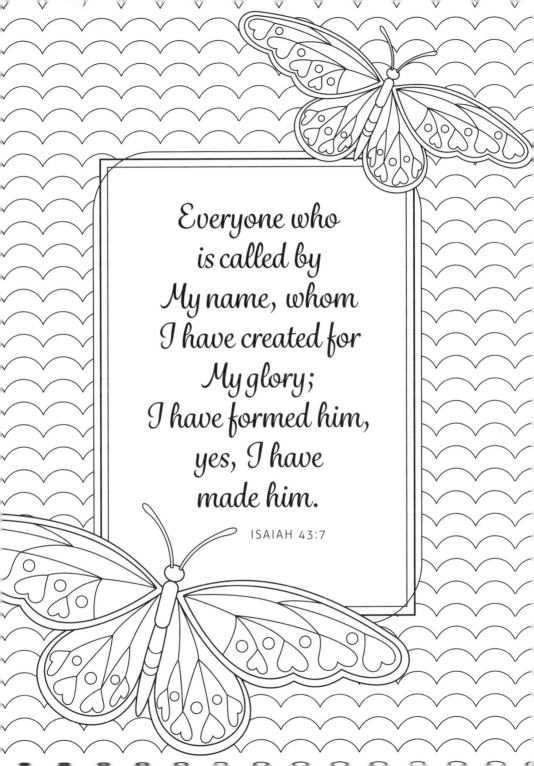

Everyone who
is called by
My name, whom
I have created for
My glory;
I have formed him,
yes, I have
made him.

ISAIAH 43:7

Lord, I want to live my life the way You want me to every day. Help me not to be stuck in my past, or so geared toward the future that I miss the richness of the present. Help me to experience the wealth in each moment. I don't desire to take a single step apart from Your presence. If You're not moving me, I'm staying here until I have a leading from You. I know I can only get to the future You have for me by walking one step at a time in Your will today. In Jesus' name I pray.

My Prayer

Lord, teach me to value each moment. ....

....

....

....

....

....

....

....

....

....

....

....

....

....

This is
the day the
Lord has made;
we will
rejoice and be
glad in it.

PSALM 118:24

Thank You, Father God, that when I need hope, You are my *Hope* (Psalm 71:5). When I am weak, You are my *Strength* (Isaiah 12:2). When I am weary, You are my *Resting Place* (Jeremiah 50:6). When I need freedom, You are my *Deliverer* (Psalm 70:5). When I want guidance, You are my *Counselor* (Psalm 16:7). When I need healing, You are my *Healer* (Malachi 4:2). When I seek protection, You are my *Shield* (Psalm 33:20). When I am going through a difficult time, You are my *Stronghold in the Day of Trouble* (Nahum 1:7). I am privileged and glad to receive all You have promised Your children. Thank You for being my heavenly Father and the answer to my every need. In Jesus' name I pray.

SHIELD
RESTING PLACE
STRONGHOLD
DELIVERER
COUNSELOR
HEALER
STRENGTH
HOPE

Lord, I want to know You more.

My Prayer

Lord, I want to know You more. ....
....
....
....
....
....
....
....
....
....
....
....
....
....
....
....
....
....
....
....
....

SHIELD
STRONGHOLD
DELIVERER
RESTING PLACE
COUNSELOR
HEALER STRENGTH
HOPE

Behold
what manner of
love the Father
has bestowed on us,
that we should be
called children
of God!

1 JOHN 3:1

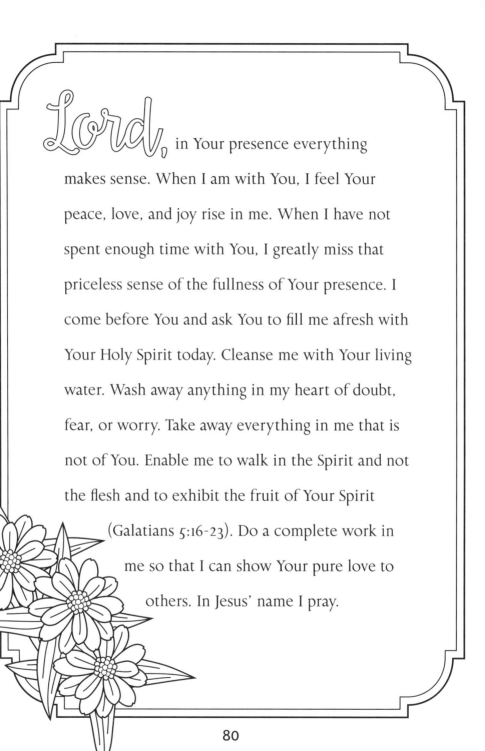

Lord, in Your presence everything makes sense. When I am with You, I feel Your peace, love, and joy rise in me. When I have not spent enough time with You, I greatly miss that priceless sense of the fullness of Your presence. I come before You and ask You to fill me afresh with Your Holy Spirit today. Cleanse me with Your living water. Wash away anything in my heart of doubt, fear, or worry. Take away everything in me that is not of You. Enable me to walk in the Spirit and not the flesh and to exhibit the fruit of Your Spirit (Galatians 5:16-23). Do a complete work in me so that I can show Your pure love to others. In Jesus' name I pray.

My Prayer

Lord, touch me with Your Holy Spirit. ....

....

....

....

....

....

....

....

....

....

....

....

....

....

The Spirit
Himself bears
witness with our
spirit that we
are children
of God.

ROMANS 8:16

Lord, I am grateful for Your Word. It shows me how to live, and I realize my life only works if I'm living Your way. Meet me there in the pages and teach me what I need to know. "Open my eyes, that I may see wondrous things from Your law" (Psalm 119:18). Thank You for the comfort, healing, deliverance, and peace Your Word brings me. It is food for my starving soul. Help me to read it every day so that I have a solid understanding of who You are, who You made me to be, and how I am to live. May Your words live in me so that when I pray, I will see answers to my prayers (John 15:7). In Jesus' name I pray.

My Prayer

Lord, guide me with Your Word. ....
....
....
....
....
....
....
....
....
....
....
....
....
....
....
....
....

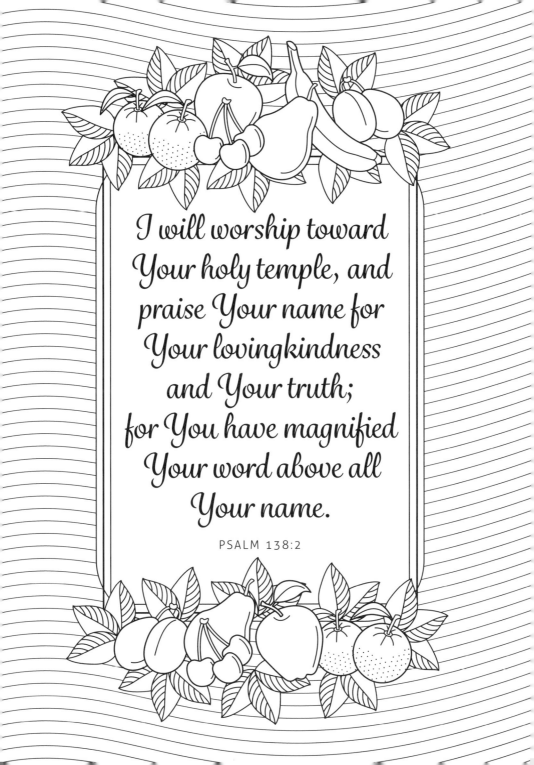

I will worship toward Your holy temple, and praise Your name for Your lovingkindness and Your truth; for You have magnified Your word above all Your name.

PSALM 138:2

Lord, I enter Your gates with thanksgiving, and Your courts with praise (Psalm 100:4). I worship You as the almighty, all-powerful God of heaven and earth, and the Creator of all things. No one is greater than You. I praise You as my heavenly Father, who is with me every day to guide and protect me. Thank You for all You have given me, and all You will provide for me in the future. "You guard all that is mine. The land you have given me is a pleasant land" (Psalm 16:5-6 NLT). I praise You for Your love that liberates me and makes me whole.

Pour Your love into me so that it overflows to others and glorifies You in the process.

In Jesus' name I pray.

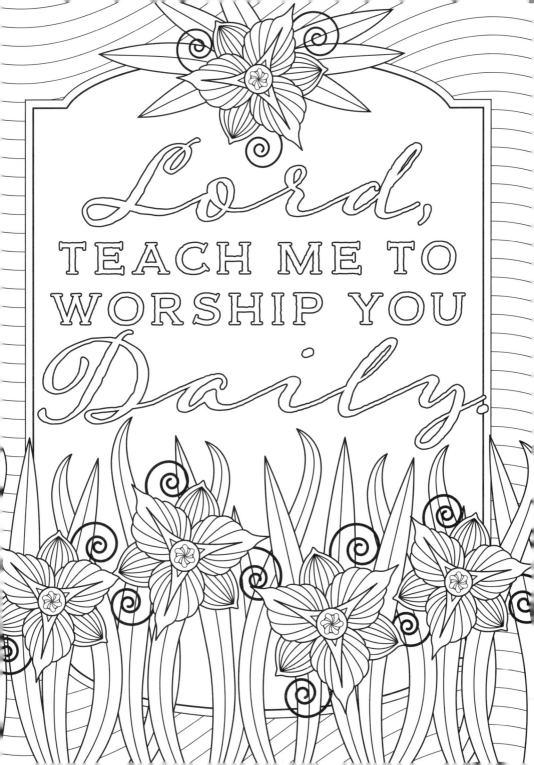

My Prayer

Lord, teach me to worship You daily. ....

....

....

....

....

....

....

....

....

....

....

....

....

....

....

....

....

....

....

....

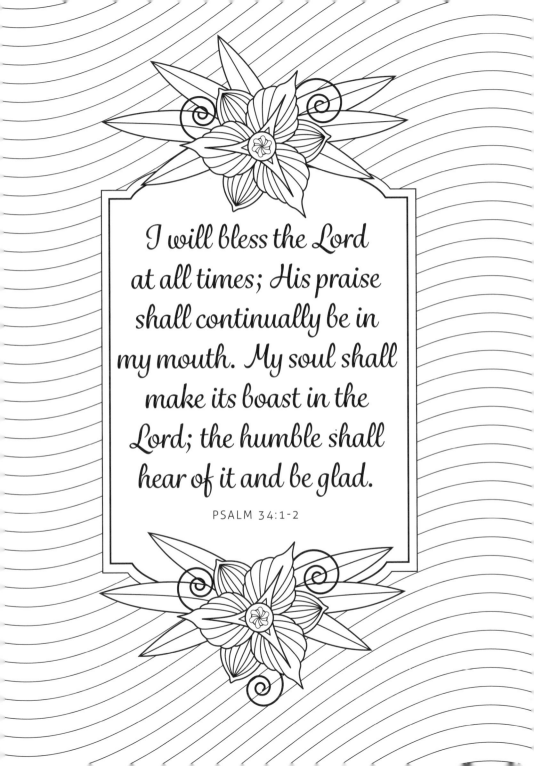

I will bless the Lord at all times; His praise shall continually be in my mouth. My soul shall make its boast in the Lord; the humble shall hear of it and be glad.

PSALM 34:1-2

Lord, I know Your judgments are perfect, and so I will praise You above all things—even my own desires and expectations. You are my Resting Place and the Solid Rock on which I stand. Nothing will shake me, not even seemingly unanswered prayers. When I can't see the answers to my prayers, open my eyes to see things from Your perspective. "I will lift up my eyes to the hills—from whence comes my help? My help comes from the LORD, who made heaven and earth" (Psalm 121:1-2). I am grateful that You, who are the all-powerful, all-knowing God of the universe, are also my heavenly Father, who loves me unconditionally and will never forsake me. Thank You for hearing and answering my prayers. In Jesus' name I pray.

My Prayer

Lord, I will trust in You. ....
....
....
....
....
....
....
....
....
....
....
....
....
....
....
....

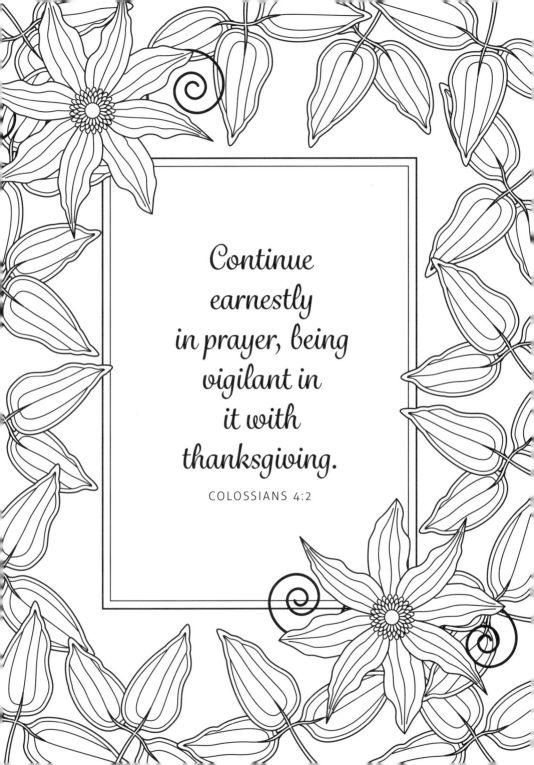

Continue
earnestly
in prayer, being
vigilant in
it with
thanksgiving.

COLOSSIANS 4:2

Lord, I come humbly before You and seek Your kingdom and Your dominion in my heart and life above all else. May Your kingdom be established wherever I go and in whatever I do. Make me a pure vessel for Your power to go forth and proclaim the rule of King Jesus where You have given me influence and opportunity to do so. Thank You, Lord, for Your many gifts to me. Thank You for Your gifts of salvation, justification, righteousness, eternal life, and grace. Thank You for Your gifts of love, peace, and joy. Thank You that these will never fail in my life because You are my everlasting Father and *You* will never fail. In Jesus' name I pray.

My Prayer

Lord, help me to seek Your kingdom. ....

....

....

....

....

....

....

....

....

....

....

....

....

....

....

....

Do not fear, little flock, for it is your Father's good pleasure to give you the kingdom.

LUKE 12:32

Lord,

You are everything to me. I know that because of You I am never without love, joy, hope, power, protection, and provision. Because of You I can rise above my limitations and live in peace, knowing You will work things out for my good as I live Your way. Help me to read Your Word every day. Open my eyes more and more to Your truth. Enable me to recognize and understand Your promises to me so that I can daily choose to reject all doubt in my life. I acknowledge You in all my ways and depend on You to direct my path (Proverbs 3:5-6). Help me to trust You in all things every day. Keep me from doubting You and Your Word. In Jesus' name I pray.

My Prayer

Lord, work things out for my good. ....

....

....

....

....

....

....

....

....

....

....

....

....

....

....

....

....

....

We know
that all things work
together for good to
those who love God,
to those who are the
called according to
His purpose.

ROMANS 8:28

Lord, I pray You would teach me to do Your will (Psalm 143:10). Work the desire for Your will into my heart (Philippians 2:13). Help me to "stand perfect and complete" in Your will and stay in the center of it at all times (Colossian 4:12). I am grateful to You that Your will can be known. Guide my every step so that I don't make a wrong decision or take a wrong path. "I delight to do Your will, O my God" (Psalm 40:8). Fill me with the knowledge of Your will in all wisdom and spiritual understanding (Colossians 1:9). Line the desires of my heart up with the desires of Your heart. I want what You want for my life.

In Jesus' name I pray.

My Prayer

Lord, I delight to do Your will. ....

....

....

....

....

....

....

....

....

....

....

....

....

....

....

....

This is the confidence that we have in Him, that if we ask anything according to His will, He hears us.

1 JOHN 5:14

Lord, I commit my work to You.
I pray that I will always be in Your will in whatever I do, and that I will do it well. I pray that all I do is pleasing to You and to those for whom and with whom I am working. Fulfill my purpose for Your pleasure and Your glory (Psalm 90:17). Help me to understand what is the hope of my calling (Ephesians 1:17-18). Enable me to "be steadfast, immovable, always abounding in the work of the Lord" that You have given me to do, knowing that my "labor is not in vain in the Lord"—as long as it is *from* You and *for* You (1 Corinthians 15:58). In Jesus' name I pray.

My Prayer

Lord, fulfill my purpose. ....
....
....
....
....
....
....
....
....
....
....
....
....
....
....
....

May He
grant you
according to
your heart's desire,
and fulfill
all your
purpose.

PSALM 20:4

LORD,

I thank You that You are the God of love. Thank You for loving me even before I knew You (Romans 5:8). Thank You for sending Your Son, Jesus, to die for me and take upon Himself all that I deserve. Thank You, Jesus, that You have given me life with You forever, and a better life now. Your love heals me and makes me whole. "You are my Lord, my goodness is nothing apart from You" (Psalm 16:2). I know that great healing and wholeness can happen only in the presence of Your love. Enable me to open up to Your love working in my life like never before. Wash over me with Your love today. In Jesus' name I pray.

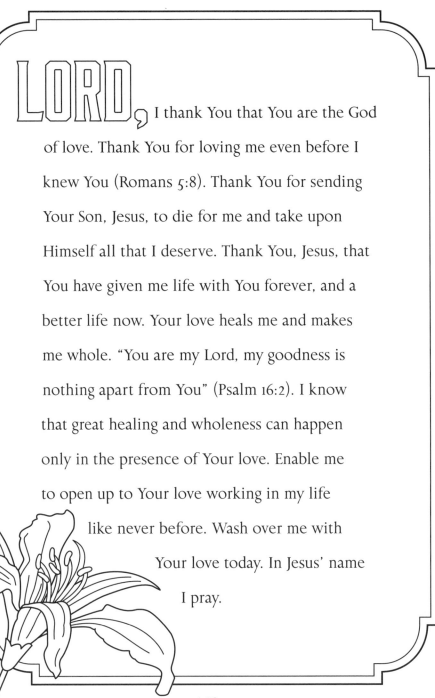

My Prayer

Lord, fill my heart with Your great love. ....

....

....

....

....

....

....

....

....

....

....

....

....

....

....

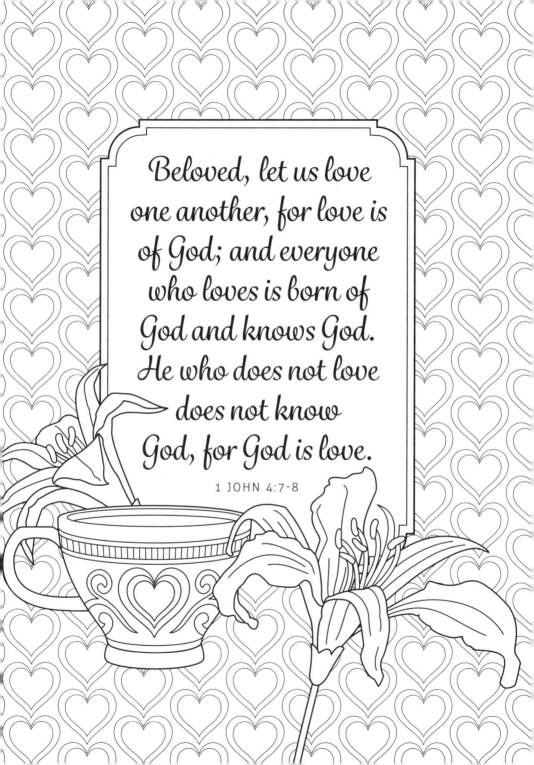

Beloved, let us love one another, for love is of God; and everyone who loves is born of God and knows God. He who does not love does not know God, for God is love.

1 JOHN 4:7-8

Lord, in You I put all my hope and expectations. "I will hope continually, and will praise You yet more and more" (Psalm 71:14). I know I have no hope without You (Ephesians 2:12), so my hope is entirely in You (Psalm 39:7). "For You are my hope, O Lord GOD; You are my trust from my youth" (Psalm 71:5). In the times I am tempted to feel hopeless—especially when I don't see answers to my prayers for a long time and I become discouraged—help me to put my eyes back on You. Enable me to end all feelings of hopelessness in my life. Help me to see they are not true and that only Your Word is true. In Jesus' name I pray.

Lord, Teach Me to Hope Only in You.

My Prayer

Lord, teach me to hope only in You. ....

....

....

....

....

....

....

....

....

....

....

....

....

....

....

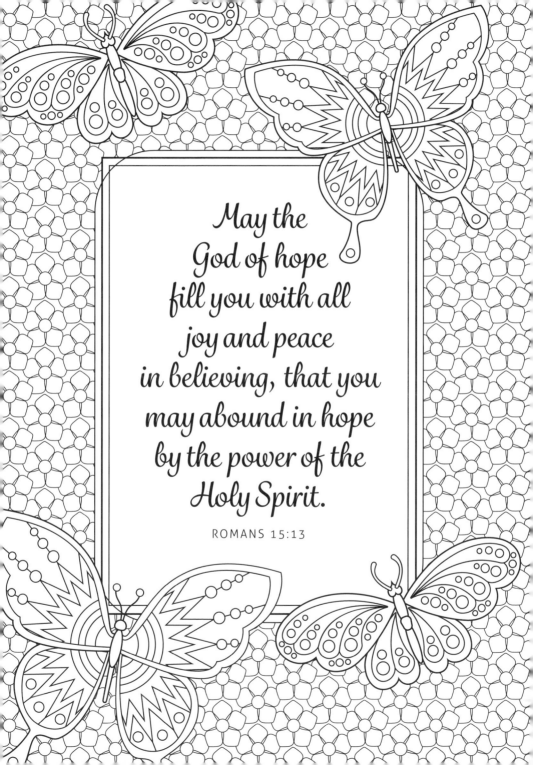

May the
God of hope
fill you with all
joy and peace
in believing, that you
may abound in hope
by the power of the
Holy Spirit.

ROMANS 15:13

Lord, help me to speak words that lift up and not tear down, words that compliment instead of criticize, words that speak unconditional love and not human expectations, and words that instill confidence and not uneasiness. Help me to have such faith in Your control in my life that I can "do all things without complaining and disputing" (Philippians 2:14). Where I have said words that are negative about myself or anyone else, forgive me. I want to be kind with my words and to daily remember that "the tongue of the wise promotes health" (Proverbs 12:18). Fill me afresh with Your Holy Spirit and pour into my heart Your love, peace, and joy. Help me to treat myself and others with respect, patience, and love. In Jesus' name I pray.

Lord, HELP ME BE *Wise* WITH MY *Words.*

My Prayer

Lord, help me be wise with my words. ....

....

....

....

....

....

....

....

....

....

....

....

....

....

....

....

The Lord God
has given Me the
tongue of the learned,
that I should know
how to speak a word
in season to him
who is weary.

ISAIAH 50:4

Lord, "who is like You, glorious in holiness?" (Exodus 15:11). You are mighty and have done great things for me. Holy is Your name (Luke 1:49). Help me to continually maintain a humble heart of worship before You. Purify my heart and mind so that I can be a partaker of Your holiness (Hebrews 12:10). You are worthy of all praise and honor and glory, for only You are holy. "O LORD, You are my God. I will exalt You, I will praise Your name, for You have done wonderful things" (Isaiah 25:1). I sing praise to You, Lord, and give thanks at the remembrance of Your holy name (Psalm 30:4). I worship You in the beauty of Your holiness (Psalm 29:2). In Jesus' name I pray.

My Prayer

Lord, I want to be holy as You are holy. ....

....

....

....

....

....

....

....

....

....

....

....

....

....

....

He chose
us in Him before the
foundation of the
world, that we should
be holy and
without blame
before Him
in love.

EPHESIANS 1:4

Lord, I am grateful for Your power extended to me. You have shown Yourself strong on my behalf countless times because my heart is loyal to You (2 Chronicles 16:9). By Your great and almighty power You have saved and redeemed me (Nehemiah 1:10). You have delivered me, protected me, and provided for me, and I know You will continue to do so. You uphold all things by the word of Your power (Hebrews 1:3). Thank You that because You are all-powerful, that means all things are possible. Therefore I refuse to become discouraged or fearful about any aspect of my life. I will not trust in the wisdom of man, but I will trust in You and Your perfect wisdom and power. In Jesus' name I pray.

My Prayer

Lord, cause Your power to work in my life. ....

....

....

....

....

....

....

....

....

....

....

....

....

....

....

....

....

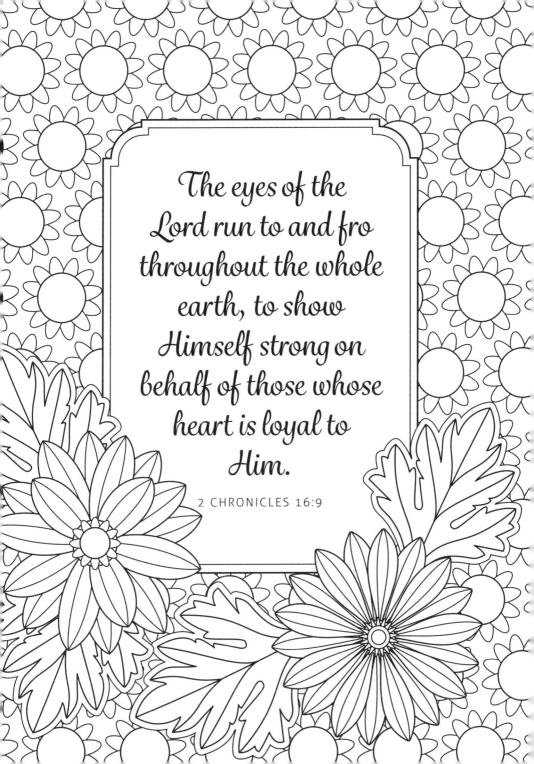

The eyes of the Lord run to and fro throughout the whole earth, to show Himself strong on behalf of those whose heart is loyal to Him.

2 CHRONICLES 16:9

Lord, my hope is in You, and I know You will never fail me. Thank You that Your restoration is ongoing in my life. I am grateful that I am Your child and You have given me a purpose. Thank You for the great future You have for me because You love me (1 Corinthians 2:9). Thank You that I am complete in You (Colossians 2:10). Thank You that I am never alone (Matthew 28:20). Help me to not think of giving up when things become difficult. Help me to remember that even in hard times You will help me persevere. Keep me from becoming discouraged in times of waiting. I know Your timing is perfect and the way You do things is right. In Jesus' name I pray.

My Prayer

Lord, in You I will not be shaken. ....

....

....

....

....

....

....

....

....

....

....

....

....

....

....

....

....

....

....

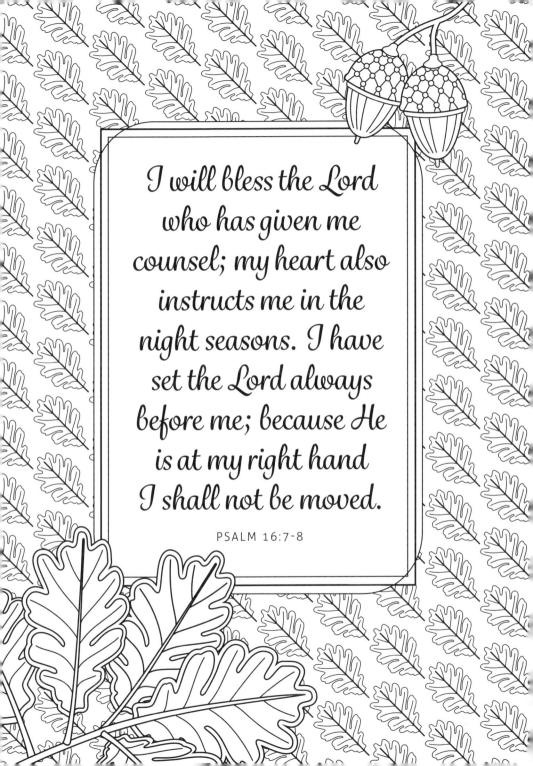

I will bless the Lord who has given me counsel; my heart also instructs me in the night seasons. I have set the Lord always before me; because He is at my right hand I shall not be moved.

PSALM 16:7-8

Lord, I don't want to stop up the flow of Your blessings in my life by not giving when and where I should. I am grateful for all You have given me, but I pray I will not merely give to get, but give only to please You. Help me to understand the release that happens in my life when I give so that I can let go of things. Help me to "not forget to do good and to share," for I know that with such sacrifices You are "well pleased" (Hebrews 13:16). Help me to give and thereby store up treasures in heaven that do not fail, for I know that where my treasure is, my heart will be there also (Luke 12:33-34). In Jesus' name I pray.

My Prayer

Lord, help me to be a cheerful giver. ....

....

....

....

....

....

....

....

....

....

....

....

....

....

....

....

....

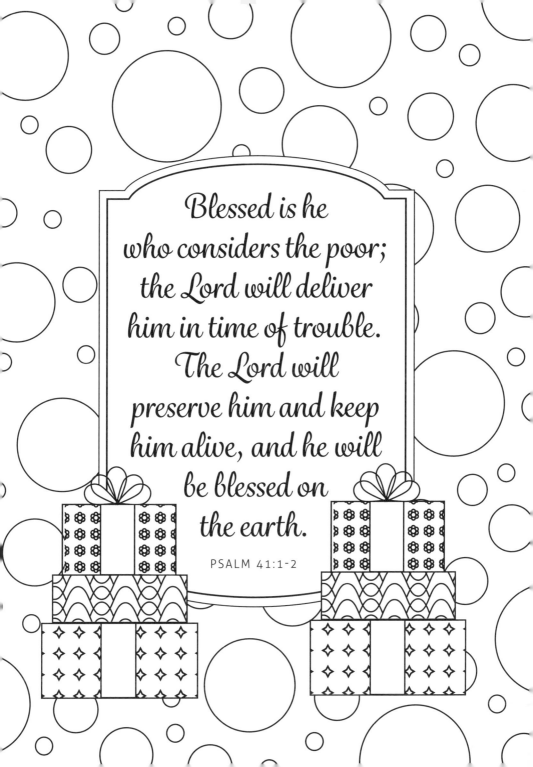

Blessed is he
who considers the poor;
the Lord will deliver
him in time of trouble.
The Lord will
preserve him and keep
him alive, and he will
be blessed on
the earth.

PSALM 41:1-2

Lord, I know Your thoughts toward me are of peace, to give me a future and a hope (Jeremiah 29:11). I know that You have saved me and called me with a holy calling, not according to my works, but according to Your own purpose and grace (2 Timothy 1:9). Thank You, Holy Spirit, that You are always with me and will guide me on the path so that I won't lose my way. Move me into powerful ministry that will impact the lives of others for Your kingdom and Your glory. I reach out for Your hand today so I can walk with You into the future You have for me. In Jesus' name I pray.

My Prayer

Lord, lead me into my future. ....
....
....
....
....
....
....
....
....
....
....
....
....
....
....

Those who are planted in the house of the Lord shall flourish in the courts of our God. They shall still bear fruit in old age; they shall be fresh and flourishing, to declare that the Lord is upright.

PSALM 92:13-15

Stormie Omartian

is the bestselling author (more than 35 million books sold) of The Power of a Praying®series, plus *Lead Me, Holy Spirit*; *Prayer Warrior*; *Choose Love*; and *Out of Darkness*. Stormie and her husband, Michael, have been married more than 40 years. They are the parents of two married children and have two granddaughters.

www.stormieomartian.com

For information on more Harvest House coloring books for adults, please visit

www.harvesthousepublishers.com

HARVEST HOUSE PUBLISHERS
EUGENE, OREGON